Contents

Stop! Look! Listen!

Before you begin...

You will need:

1 a sharpened pencil
2 paper
3 an eraser
4 a pencil sharpener
5 colored pencils, markers or crayons
6 a comfortable place to sit and draw
7 a good light source

Let's draw cartoon people!

No Rules!

This book is designed to teach the basics of drawing cartoon people. There are no rules about cartooning, so you can spend hours just sketching, doodling and playing with different shapes. Just have fun!

Sketch, doodle, play!

If the instructions tell you to use an oval to draw a nose and you want to use a triangle...draw a triangle. Cartooning is all about having fun drawing. Experiment, try out some crazy ideas. If it makes you and your friends smile, or giggle, or even laugh out loud, you're doing it right!

A few cartooning tips

1   Draw lightly at first—SKETCH, so you can erase extra lines.
2   Practice, practice, practice!
3   Have fun cartooning!

Basic Shapes and Lines

Here are some basic shapes and lines you will use to draw cartoon people:

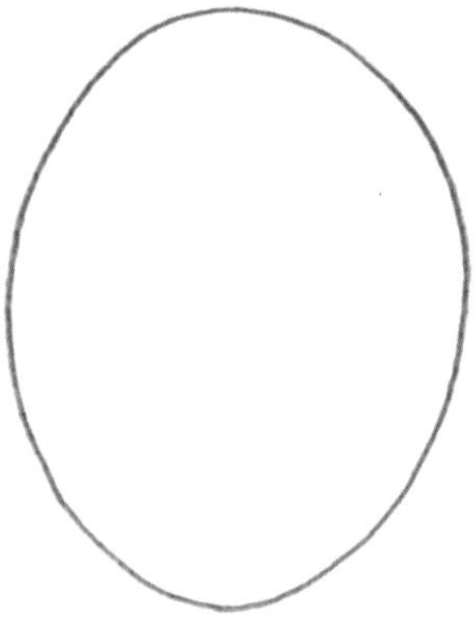

Oval

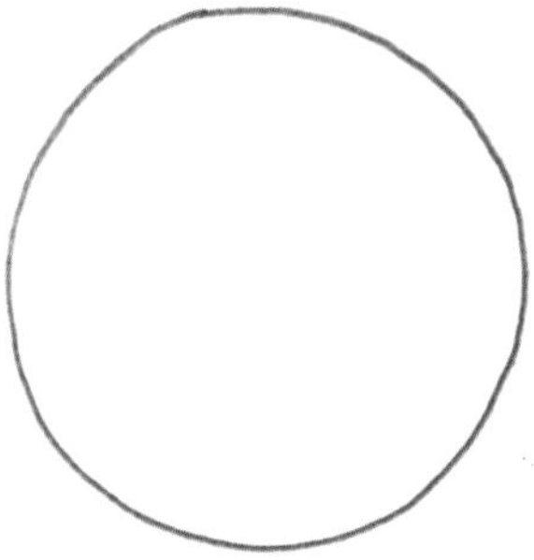

Circle

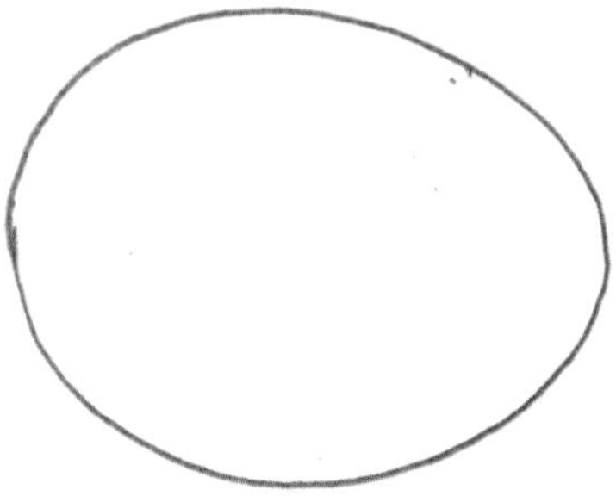

Egg

Rectangle

Square

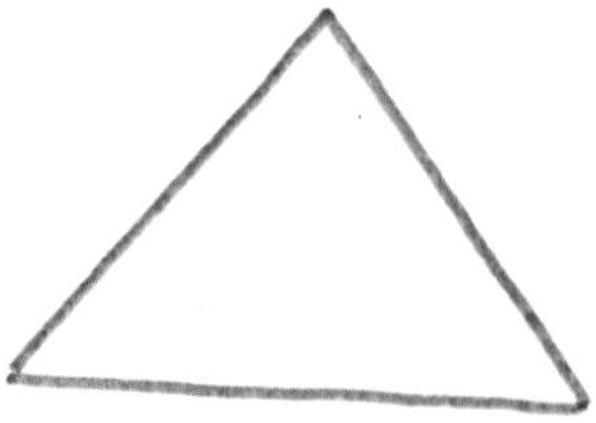

Triangle

Straight lines

Squiggly lines

Curved lines

Heads (Front View)

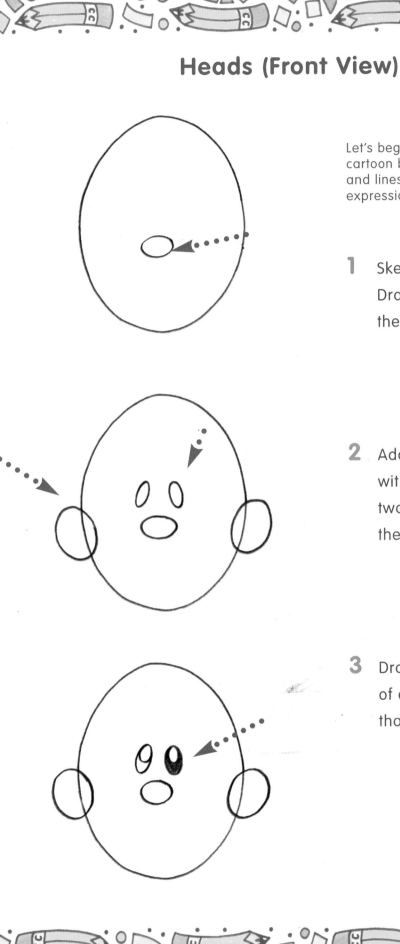

Let's begin by drawing a front view of a cartoon boy's head. Using basic shapes and lines, we will create a unique expression for our cartoon character.

1 Sketch an **oval** for the head. Draw a small **oval** inside it for the nose.

2 Add two **egg** shapes, level with the nose, for ears. Draw two **ovals** above the nose for the eyes.

3 Draw a small **oval** at the top of each eye. Darken around that oval in both eyes.

4 Draw a **curved line** for the mouth. Add a **straight line**, on each side of the mouth, for a smile.

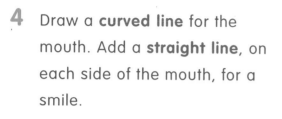

5 Draw a half **circle**, on the top of the head, for hair. Add a few **curved lines** for hair strands.

6 LOOK at the final drawing! Erase extra sketch lines. Darken the final lines. Add color!

Good Job!

Heads (Side View)

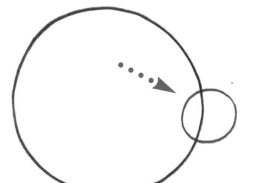

People come in all shapes and sizes, so let's draw a chubby face this time.

1 Sketch a **circle** for the head. Sketch a small **circle** for the nose.

2 Draw an **oval**, with a smaller **oval** inside, for the eye. Darken around the smaller oval.

Draw a partial **oval** for the ear.

3 Draw two **curved lines** for the smiling mouth.

4 Draw an **egg** shape around his ear for hair. Add a tilted **oval** for an eyebrow.

5 LOOK at the final drawing! Erase extra sketch lines. Darken the final lines. Color your Grandpop.

WOW! You drew a great Grandpop's face!

Hair

Hair can make a huge difference in a cartoon character's appearance.

Look at these samples of different hair styles drawn on the same face. Can you see how the hair changes the entire character?

Let's create some hair styles...

Curly Hair

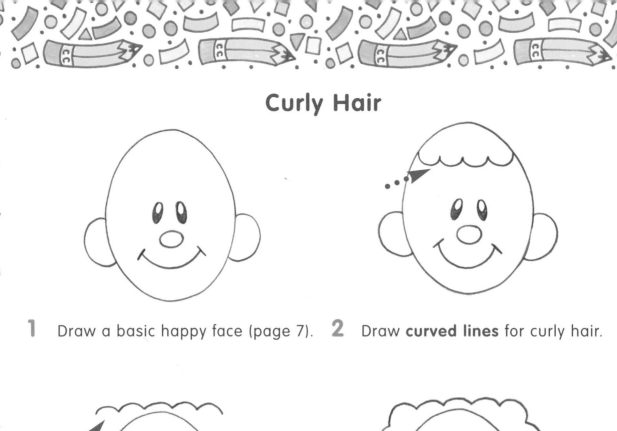

1 Draw a basic happy face (page 7).

2 Draw **curved lines** for curly hair.

3 Add more **curved lines**.

4 Add more **curved lines** around the head, connecting to the ears.

5 Add more **curved lines**.

6 Erase extra sketch lines. Darken the final lines. Add color!

More Curly Hair

1 Draw a happy face with half an **oval** for a pug nose.

2 Add **curved** hair **lines** on top of the head.

3 Draw more **curved** hair **lines** on top.

4 Add more on each side.

5 Draw more **curved lines** around the face.

6 Erase extra sketch lines. Darken the final lines. Add color!

Straight Hair

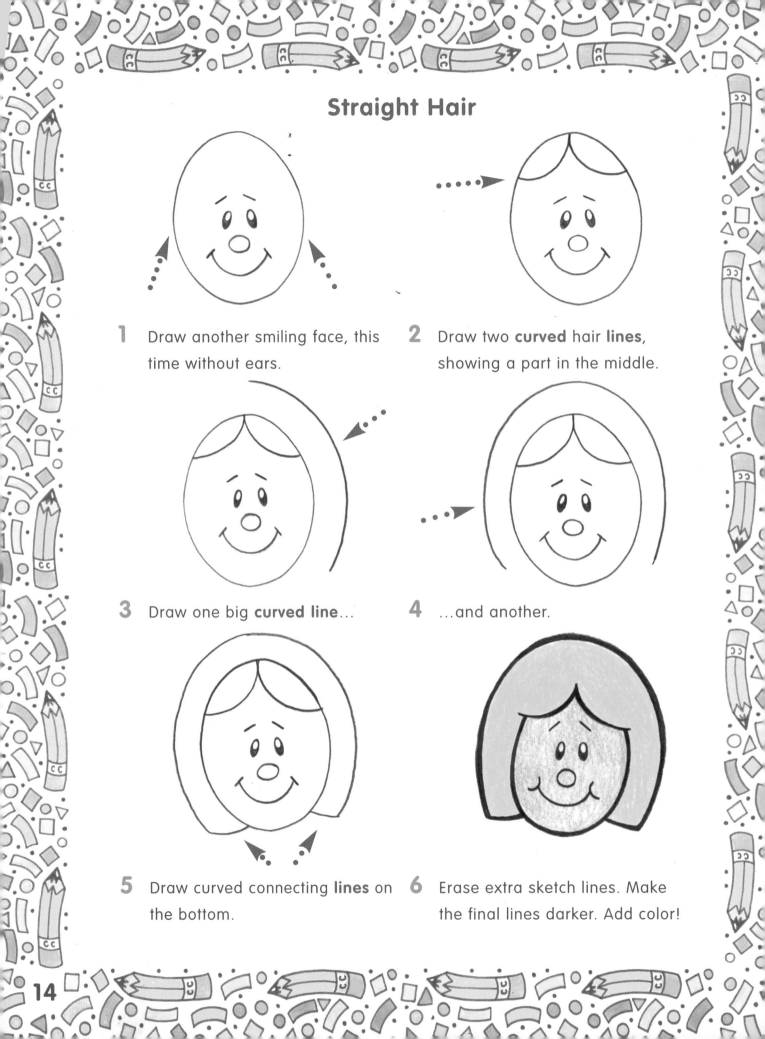

1 Draw another smiling face, this time without ears.

2 Draw two **curved** hair **lines**, showing a part in the middle.

3 Draw one big **curved line**…

4 …and another.

5 Draw curved connecting **lines** on the bottom.

6 Erase extra sketch lines. Make the final lines darker. Add color!

14

Hair Magic

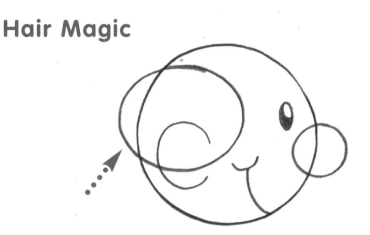

1 Sketch the side view of a chubby face (page 9).

2 Sketch an **oval** overlapping the ear. Looks like a chubby bald man, doesn't it?

3 Sketch an overlapping **oval** on top of the head.

4 Sketch a **circle** overlapping the ovals.

5 LOOK at the final drawing! Erase extra sketch lines. Darken the final lines. Add color!

Cool Grandmom!

Expressions and Emotions

In these drawings, can you see how eyes and mouths show feelings? Experiment with different shapes and lines when you draw mouths and eyes. Have fun! Discover for yourself what looks cool! For now, though, let's try a few basic facial expressions...

Happy

Angry

Sad

Surprised

Silly

Really Happy!

We'll start with a different face and a happy mouth...

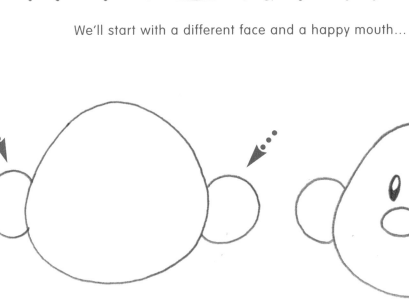

1 Sketch an oval for the head. Add two smaller ovals for the ears.

2 Sketch an **oval** nose. Draw two eyes. Darken around the bottom.

3 Draw connecting **curved lines** for the hair.

4 Add a **curved line** for a smiling mouth.

5 Draw another **curved** mouth **line**, under the top mouth line.

6 Add a **straight line** down the middle of the mouth.

7 Draw another **straight line** crossing the mouth for teeth.

8 LOOK at the final drawing! Erase extra sketch lines. Add color!

Now let's try a grumpy guy...

1 Draw the same head again, without eyes.

2 For each eye, simply draw a sideways "V."

3 Make a sideways raindrop for the mouth.

4 LOOK at the final drawing! Add two **straight lines** to the mouth. Erase extra sketch lines. Add color!

Great Grumpy Guy!

19

Quiz

What one thing changes in these four faces?

By the way, have you noticed you're holding the book upside down?

Answer: The mouth.

Look at your face in the mirror. Make a funny face with a funny mouth.
Now draw **your** funny face!

20

1 Draw a girl's face. Add **curved lines** for eyes and an **oval** nose.

2 Draw a large **oval** for her mouth.

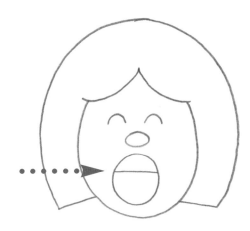

3 Add a **straight line** across the mouth.

4 Draw a **line** down the middle.

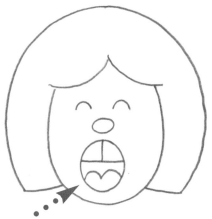

5 Draw two **curved lines** inside the bottom of the mouth.

6 LOOK at the final drawing! Add color!

Is she yawning? Yelling? Or is she singing?

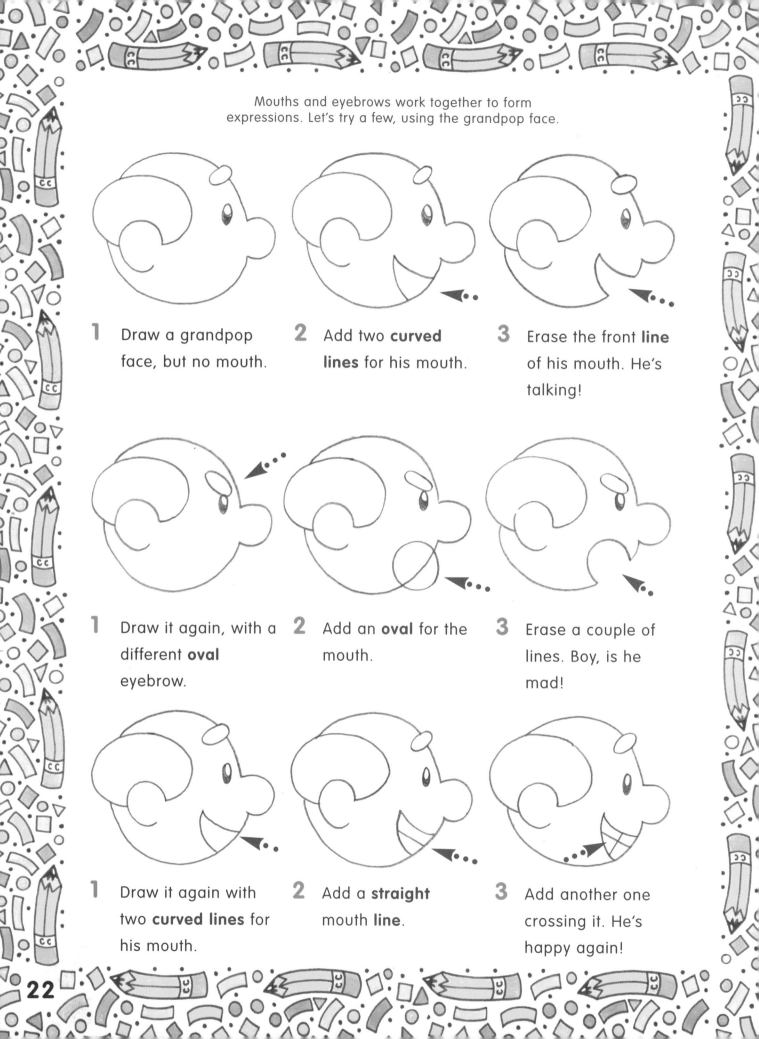

Mouths and eyebrows work together to form expressions. Let's try a few, using the grandpop face.

1 Draw a grandpop face, but no mouth.

2 Add two **curved lines** for his mouth.

3 Erase the front **line** of his mouth. He's talking!

1 Draw it again, with a different **oval** eyebrow.

2 Add an **oval** for the mouth.

3 Erase a couple of lines. Boy, is he mad!

1 Draw it again with two **curved lines** for his mouth.

2 Add a **straight** mouth **line**.

3 Add another one crossing it. He's happy again!

Eyes can make all the difference.
Let's try a few variations.

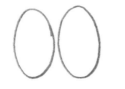

1 Draw two **ovals**.

2 Draw two smaller **ovals** inside them.

3 Draw small **circles** inside the small ovals. Darken around the circles.

4 Add some simple **lines** for eyelashes.

5 Or, draw a **line** across each eye to make them droopy.

6 Or, make one eye wink!

7 Draw this cartoon face with **big** eyes.

8 Add simple **lines** to make eyeglasses.

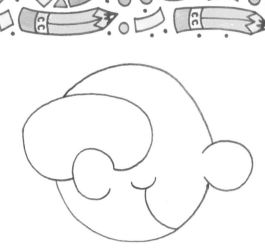

1 Draw the side view of the grandfather's head again.

2 Add a large **oval**, for the eye.

3 Draw a **circle** inside the oval eye.

4 Add a smaller **circle** inside that one.

5 Darken around the circle. Add a **curved line** at the bottom of the eye, for his cheek.

6 LOOK carefully at the final drawing. Darken the final lines. Add color!

1 Draw the grandpop's head again.

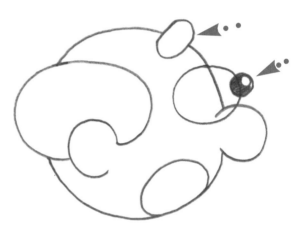

2 Sketch an **oval** for his mouth.

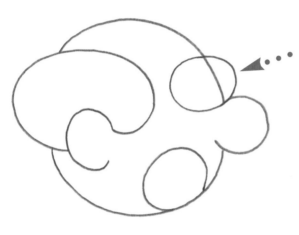

3 Sketch another **oval** for his bulging eye.

4 Draw an **oval** eyebrow. Draw the darkened eyeball.

5 LOOK at the final drawing! Erase extra lines. Shade and color.

Wow! He looks shocked. He's probably amazed at the different expressions you've learned to draw!

Simple lines in the eyes change the expression of the whole face. First, draw several cartoon faces without eyes. Then add the eyes you see below. Have a little fun: ask a friend to make different faces, and try drawing the different expressions you see using only simple lines and shapes!

Two **straight lines** across the top of the eyes make him look serious.

Two **lines** at an angle make him look mad.

Two **curved lines** on the side of the eyes makes him a little confused.

Two **curved lines** across the top of the eyes make him sad.

Eyebrows are another way to show emotions on a face. using these examples as a guide, experiment with eyebrows.

Also, look at your eyebrows in the mirror. Make different faces—happy, sad, angry. See how they change, depending on your mood.

Draw **straight lines** at an angle.

Try **triangles**! •••••

Or, try **curved lines**.

Ovals and **egg** shapes make great eyebrows too. Bend them. Or tilt them. Experiment!

Noses give you a great way to make one cartoon character look different from another.

Here are a few easy ways to draw noses. Practice these, then invent a few of your own.

It's easy to add a hat. As with noses, distinct hats can help people looking at your cartoons distinguish one character from another.

1 Draw a basic face, with a bowl shape on top for the cap.

2 Sketch a tilted **oval** (for the brim).

3 Draw a small **circle** on top.

4 Add three **curved lines**. Erase extra sketch lines.

He loves his new hat!

Hands

Cartoon hands are very important because they show communication. Most cartoon characters have three fingers and a thumb. Try drawing this open hand.

1   Sketch an **oval**

2   Sketch a smaller **oval**, for the thumb.

3   Sketch three overlapping **ovals**, for the fingers.

4   LOOK at the final hand! Erase extra sketch lines. Darken the final lines.

Good job! I've got to hand it to you!

More Hands

Look carefully at these steps, and try drawing hands in different positions.

Back of hand

Fist

Pointing hand

Arms

You can add arms to the hands using simple lines. Try drawing some of these.

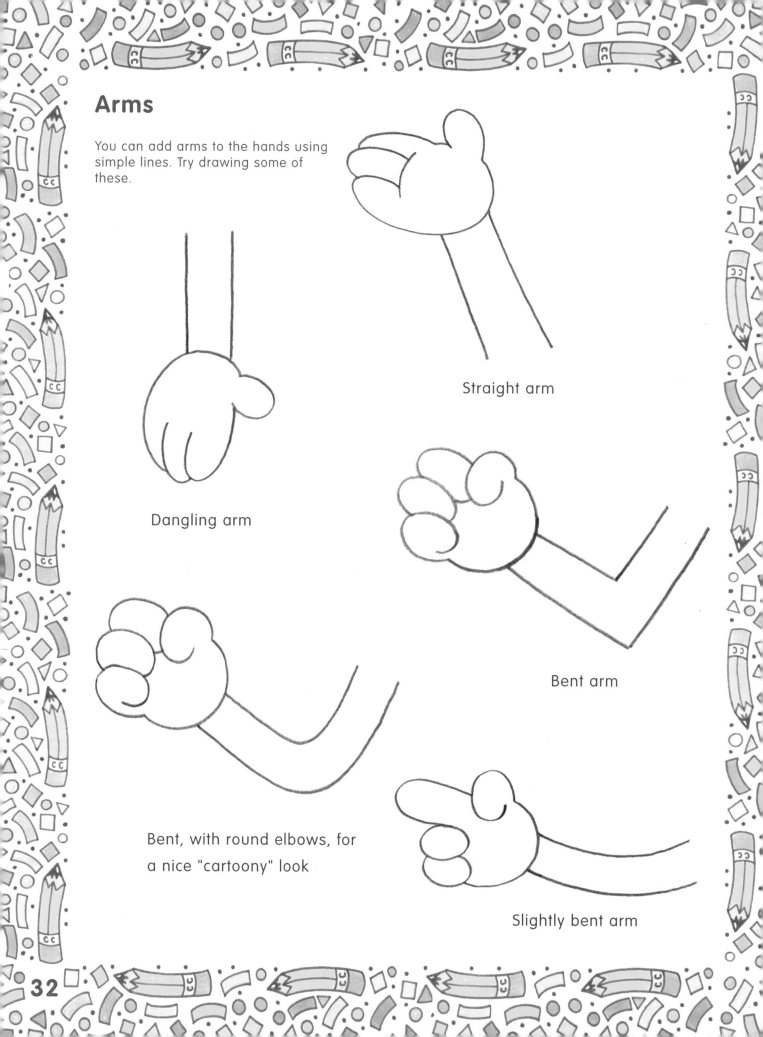

Straight arm

Dangling arm

Bent arm

Bent, with round elbows, for a nice "cartoony" look

Slightly bent arm

32

Boy

You can use ovals, circles, squares, triangles, and even rectangles to create a cartoon body. Let's draw a cartoon character—head to shoes. Draw the head at the top of the paper so you will have plenty of room for the body and legs.

1 Draw a head with hair.

Add two neck **lines**.

Sketch a large **oval** for the body.

Draw three **lines** for legs.

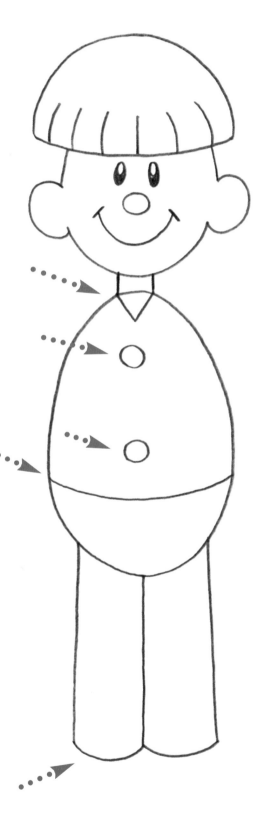

2 Draw a "V" at the bottom of the neck for a collar. Draw two small **circles** for buttons.

Add a **curved line** for the waist of his pants.

Draw two **curved lines** for the bottom of his pants.

3 For arms, draw two long **curved lines** on each side of his body.

Sketch two **ovals**, at the bottom of his legs, for feet.

4 Sketch **ovals** for his hands and fingers.

Draw a **straight line** between the shoes.

5 LOOK carefully at this drawing! Erase extra sketch lines. Darken the final lines.

Details make a BIG difference! Watch your cartoon boy change as you add details!

Add:
- freckles
- a cuff on his sleeve
- a belt and belt buckle
- pockets, with dotted lines for stitches
- shoe laces
- soles on his shoes

Great Job! Color him any color you want. It's your drawing. Be original!

Girl

Let's draw a cartoon girl with a rectangle shape for the body. Draw the head at the top of the paper, so you have room for the body and legs.

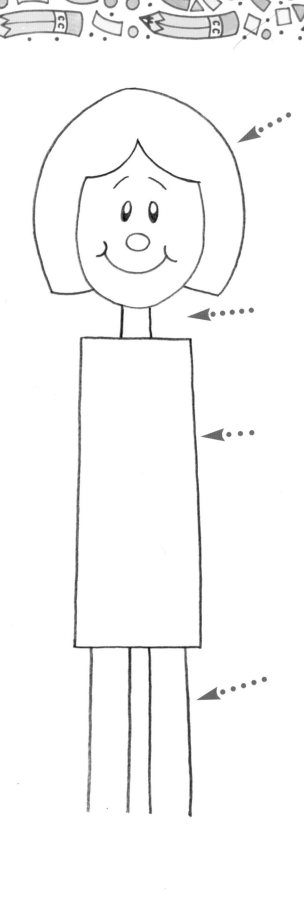

1 Draw a head with hair.

Add two neck **lines**.

Sketch a long **rectangle** for the body.

Draw four **straight lines** for legs.

2 Draw a **half-circle** for a collar.

Draw small **circles** for buttons.

Add a **line** for her waist.

Add **curved lines** on her legs for socks.

Draw two **ovals** for feet.

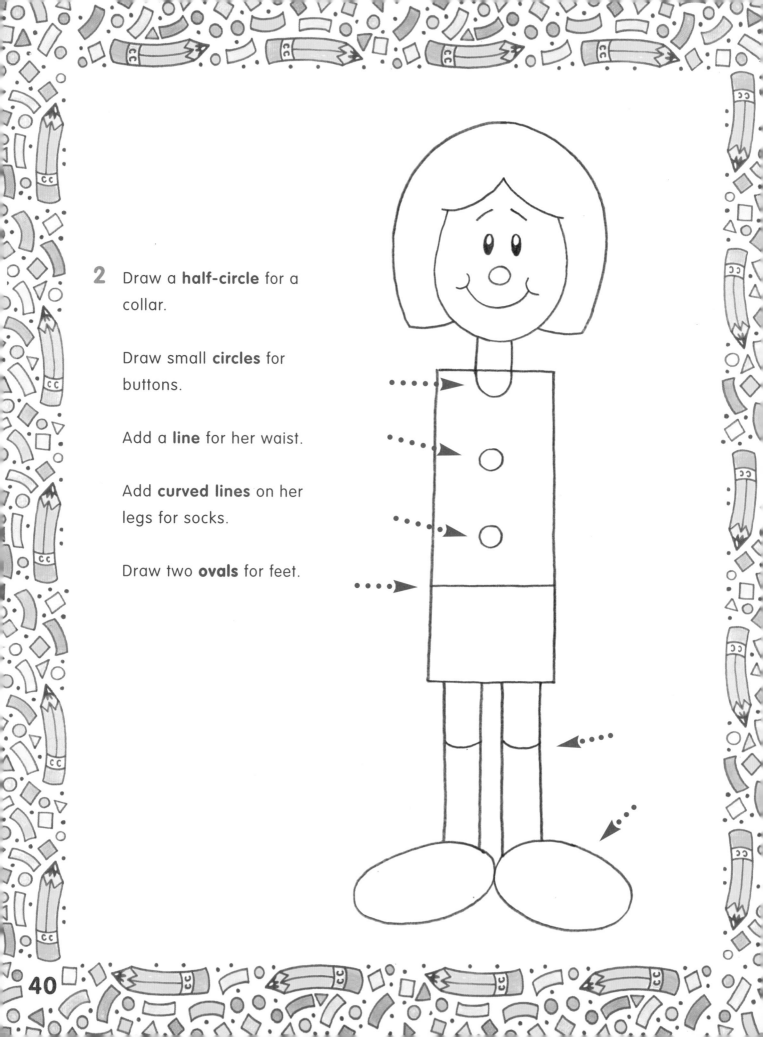

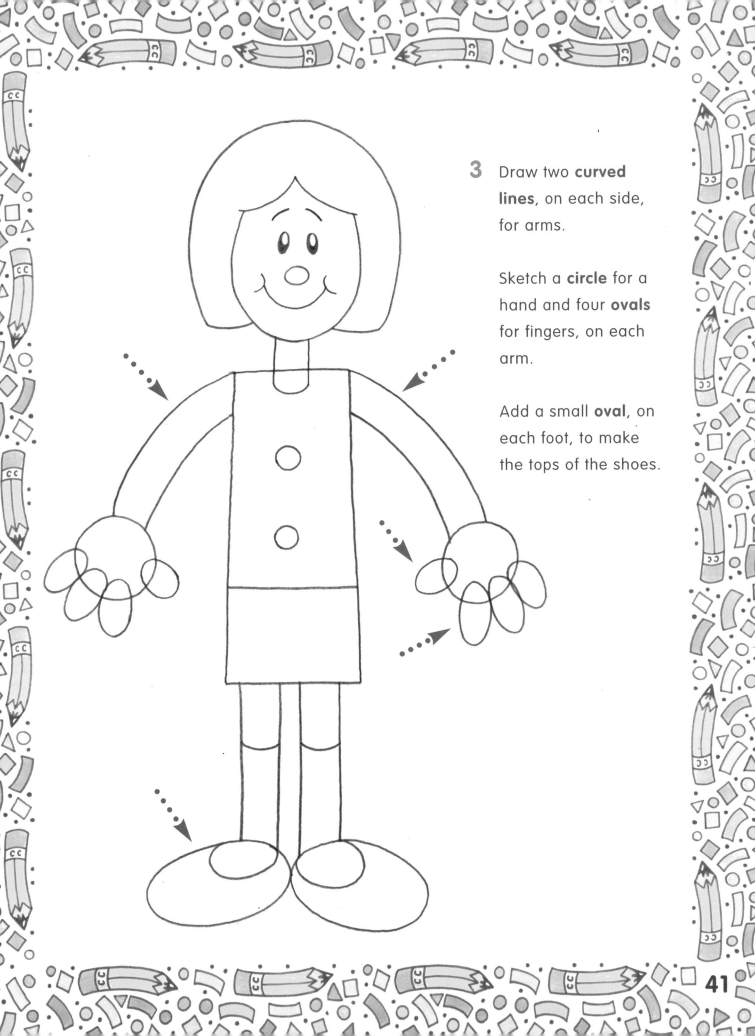

3 Draw two **curved lines**, on each side, for arms.

Sketch a **circle** for a hand and four **ovals** for fingers, on each arm.

Add a small **oval**, on each foot, to make the tops of the shoes.

4 Sketch two **circles** to begin the collar.

Add two **curved lines**, below the bottom button.

5 LOOK carefully at this drawing! Erase extra sketch lines. Darken the final lines.

She's super!

43

Let's add some details to make her more interesting.

Add:

- a small **circle** and two **triangles** for a bow
- a **circle** and three **lines** to make a wristwatch
- two **curved lines** for a bracelet

- three **straight lines** to make pleats on her skirt. Add **curved lines** on the bottom
- a crescent moon shape on each shoe
- color!

    WOW!

44

Grandpop

Remember the grandfather face you drew? Grandpop really likes extra dessert after every meal, so let's give him a chubby body.

1   Draw Grandpop's face, side view (page 9).

Sketch an upside-down **egg** shape for his body.

Sketch a **rectangle** for his legs.

Draw an **oval** for his feet.

45

2 Draw two **straight lines** for his arm.

Add a **curved line** for his waist.

Add a **line** for his other leg. Draw a **curved line** for his other foot.

3 Draw a hand.

LOOK carefully at this drawing! Erase extra lines. Darken the final lines.

Let's give Grandpop a few extra details.

Add:

- a few hair **lines**
- some eyeglasses
- a **curved line** for a pocket, so he can give you ice cream money
- dotted **lines** for seams on his pants
- **lines** for shoe laces
- soles on his shoes
- color — make him a wild dresser…why not?

Fun!

Grandmom

Let's draw Grandmom with ovals and a square to give her a cuddly body. Draw her head at the top of the paper. You will need lots of room for the body and legs.

1 Draw Grandmom's head, side view (page 15).

Sketch two overlapping **ovals** for her body.

Draw **lines** (half a square) for her dress bottom.

Draw three **straight lines** for her legs.

Sketch two **ovals** for feet.

2 Add a few **curved lines** to her hair.

Draw **lines** (a half-square) for a sleeve.

Add two **straight lines** for her arm.

Draw a hand.

Draw **curved lines** to make the tops of her shoes.

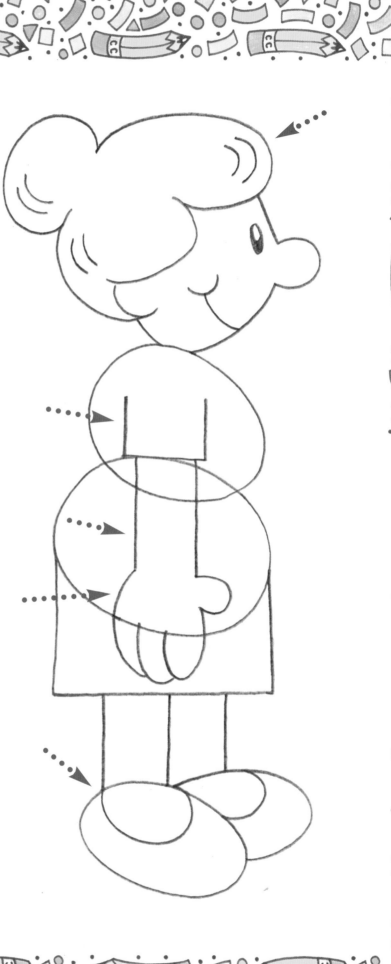

3 LOOK carefully at this drawing! Erase extra sketch lines. She's a sweetie! Let's give her some colorful accessories…

Add:

- a **line** and an **oval** for granny glasses
- an **oval** earring
- some **half-circles** for fancy lace
- two **lines** and a **circle**, on her middle finger, for a pearl ring
- more lace to the bottom of her dress
- a pattern on her dress
- two **lines** for a heel on her shoe
- color!

GREAT Grandmom!

Characters in Motion

Adding motion makes a cartoon more interesting. Let's draw a cartoon person walking. Start at the top of the paper, so you will have room for the whole body.

1 Sketch three overlapping **ovals** for the head.

Draw **lines** for the neck.

Sketch a long **oval** for the body.

Sketch two long **curved lines** for each leg.

Make **ovals** for the feet.

2 Sketch two **ovals** overlapping his head, for hair. Draw an eye. Add a mouth.

Add the **lines** for his arm. Draw a hand.

Draw a **curved line** for his waist.

Add two **curved lines** for the bottoms of his legs.

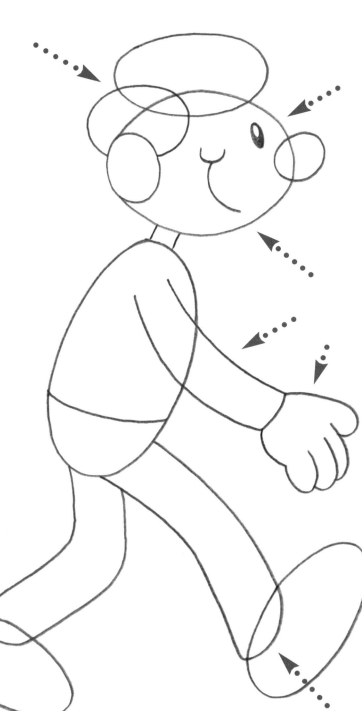

3 LOOK carefully at this drawing! Erase extra sketch lines.

How about adding some fun details…?

Add:

- hair **lines**
- an eyebrow
- a backwards "S" in his ear
- a **curved line** for a collar
- a belt
- **curved lines** on the bottom of his shoes for soles
- color!

Bravo!

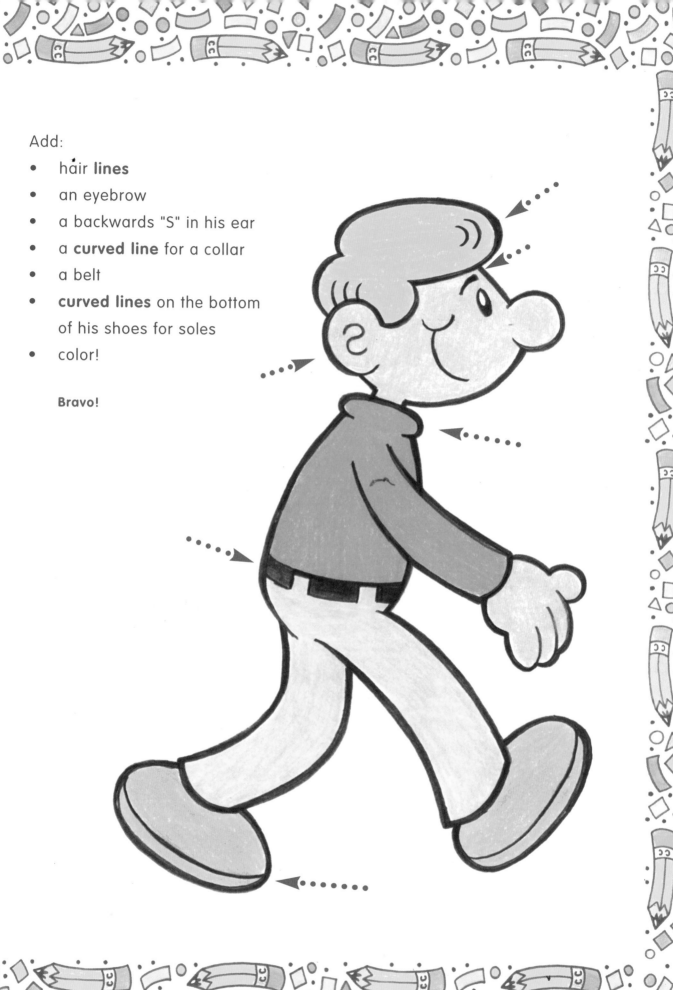

While motion makes a character interesting, lots of motion makes it even more interesting! Let's draw a cartoon character running. Remember to start at the top of the paper so you will have room for the entire body.

1 Sketch three overlapping **ovals** to make the head.

Draw two **lines** for the neck.

Sketch a tilted **rectangle** for the body.

Sketch an **oval** for the hips.

Sketch two long bent **lines** for each leg.

Sketch two **ovals** for the feet.

2 Draw two long **curved lines** for hair. Add an eye and eyebrow. Darken both. Draw **curved lines** for a smiling mouth.

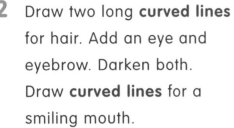

Add two long **curved lines** for an arm. Sketch a **circle** for his right arm socket.

Draw two **squares** for his running shorts.

3 Add **curved** hair **lines**.

Sketch two **ovals** for his hand.

Draw **lines** for his right arm.

Add a **curved line** on
each leg for socks.

4 Sketch three **ovals**, on his hand, for fingers.

Sketch a **circle** for his right hand. Add **curved lines** for fingers.

Add a **curved line** to his left shoe.

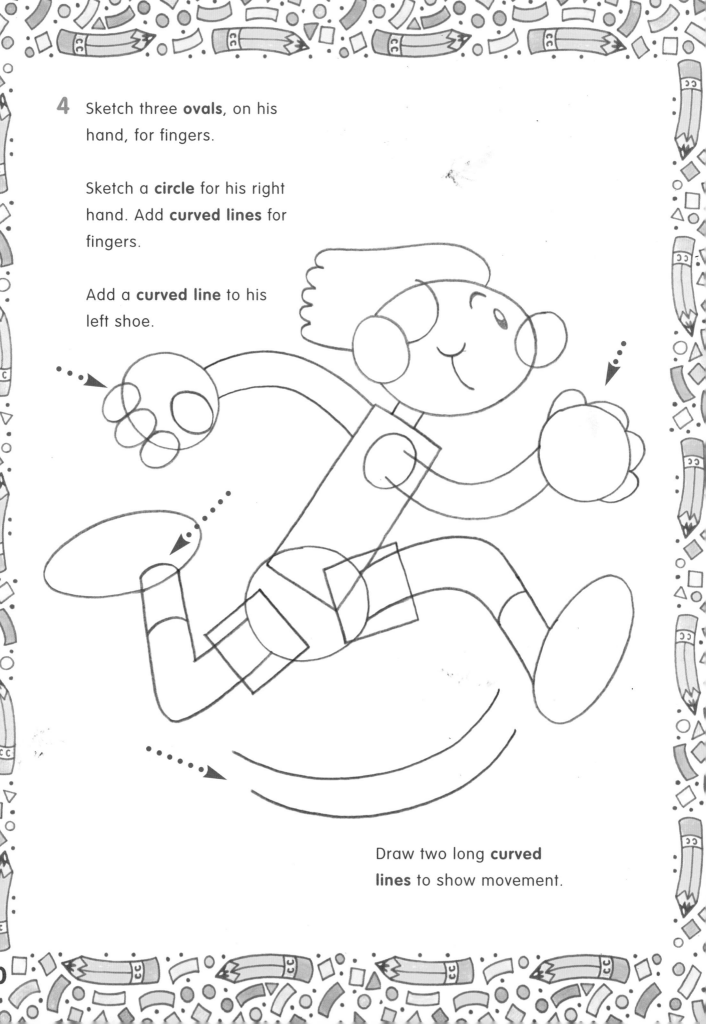

Draw two long **curved lines** to show movement.

5 LOOK carefully at this drawing! Erase extra sketch lines.

Let's add details to make him run faster...

Add:

- a large raindrop to show he's sweating
- three long **lines** to show he's fast!
- stripes on his shorts to show he's cool!
- a little cloud to show he is stirring up a little dust
- color!

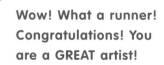

Wow! What a runner!
Congratulations! You
are a GREAT artist!

62

Award yourself! On the next page you'll find an award certificate you can photocopy to let the world know you're a **Cartoonist's Apprentice First Class! Hang it on your wall! Have fun cartooning!**

Have you enjoyed this book?

Find out about other books in this series and see sample pages online at

www.123draw.com